Discovery KIDS™

So Freaky!

LIVE. LEARN. DISCOVER.

PaRragòn

Bath · New York · Singapore · Hong Kong · Cologne · Delhi · Melbourne

First published by Parragon in 2009

Parragon
Queen Street House
4 Queen Street
Bath BA1 1HE, UK

ISBN 978-1-4075-7884-2

Printed in China

Contents

Keep Cool!

Ancient Greek leader Alexander the Great (356–323 B.C.) knew how to keep cool under pressure. When attacking Petra in present-day Jordan, he had a "secret weapon" to help him keep his cool. What was it? Work your way through the maze to find out. When you find the exit route, it will lead you to the correct answer!

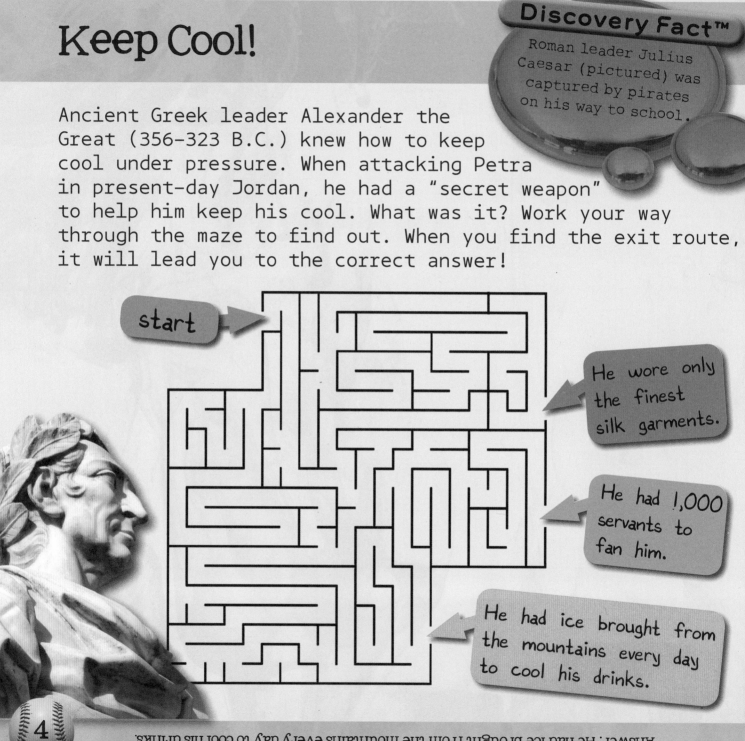

start

He wore only the finest silk garments.

He had 1,000 servants to fan him.

He had ice brought from the mountains every day to cool his drinks.

4

Intrepid Explorers!

Read around these word circles to discover the names of some of the world's most intrepid explorers. The first letter of each word is the letter in the center of the circle.

(A) This brave explorer captained the first ship to sail around the world.

Ferdinand _ _ _ _ _ _ _ _ _

(B) This famous explorer of Australia was the first European to see surfing, when he stopped in Tahiti in 1769.

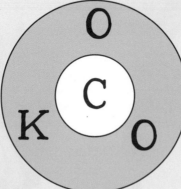

Discovery Fact™

When Christopher Columbus landed in Cuba in 1492, he thought he had landed in India!

Captain _ _ _ _ _ _ _ _ _ _

5

Big-Hearted People!

Discovery Fact™

Nurse Florence Nightingale (1820–1910) revolutionized the treatment of injured soldiers.

Throughout history there have been people who have devoted their lives to improving conditions for others. Crack the codes to discover more.

z	y	x	w	v	u	t	s	r	q	p	o	n	m	l	k	j	i	h	g	f	e	d	c	b	a
a	b	c	d	e	f	g	h	i	j	k	l	m	n	o	p	q	r	s	t	u	v	w	x	y	z

A This gentle saint (1182–1226; pictured right) saw all animals as brothers and sisters.

h	g		u	i	z	m	x	r	h		l	u		z	h	h	r	h	r

B This U.S. civil rights leader (1929–1968) was assassinated because he fought for the rights of African-American people.

n	z	i	g	r	m		o	f	g	s	v	i		p	r	m	t		q	i

C This Albanian nun (1910–1997) dedicated her life to the poor of India.

n	l	g	s	v	i		g	v	i	v	h	z

6

Babe Ruth!

George "Babe" Ruth was voted the greatest baseball player ever by *The Sporting News* in 1998. Do the math below to discover some awesome stats about his career!

A How many home runs did Ruth hit in his record-breaking 1927 season?

$$125 - (10 \times 2) - (15 \times 3) = \boxed{}$$

Answer: $\boxed{}$ home runs

B And how long did this record stand for?

$$(10 \times 2) + 9 + 5 = \boxed{}$$

Answer: $\boxed{}$ years

Olympic Star!

What did athlete Jesse Owens win four of in the track and field events at the 1936 Berlin Olympics? Unscramble the letters below to find out!

LGDO EMDLAS

_ _ _ _ _

_ _ _ _ _ _

Terrific Tennis!

Tennis player Martina Navratilova won more singles titles in her career than any other player ever. Solve the numbers below to discover exactly how many.

$$200 - (20 \times 2) + 3 + 4 = \boxed{}$$

Answer: [ ] singles titles

Crackpot Royalty!

When you have royal blood, everybody has to do what you say, so you can get away with some really weird behavior. Follow the lines to match these royals with their behavior!

A. For a time, ended every word with "peacock."

B. Collected dwarfs and giants.

C. Once forced his shoemaker to eat a pair of shoes.

1. Holy Roman Emperor Rudolf II

2. Spanish King Philip II

3. British King George III (pictured)

Answer: A.3, B.1, C.2

9

Rotten Reign!

Jean-Bedel Bokassa (1921–1996) declared himself "Emperor of Central Africa." But his reign wasn't a success! Find your way through this maze to discover what went wrong. When you find the exit route, it will lead you to the correct answer!

start

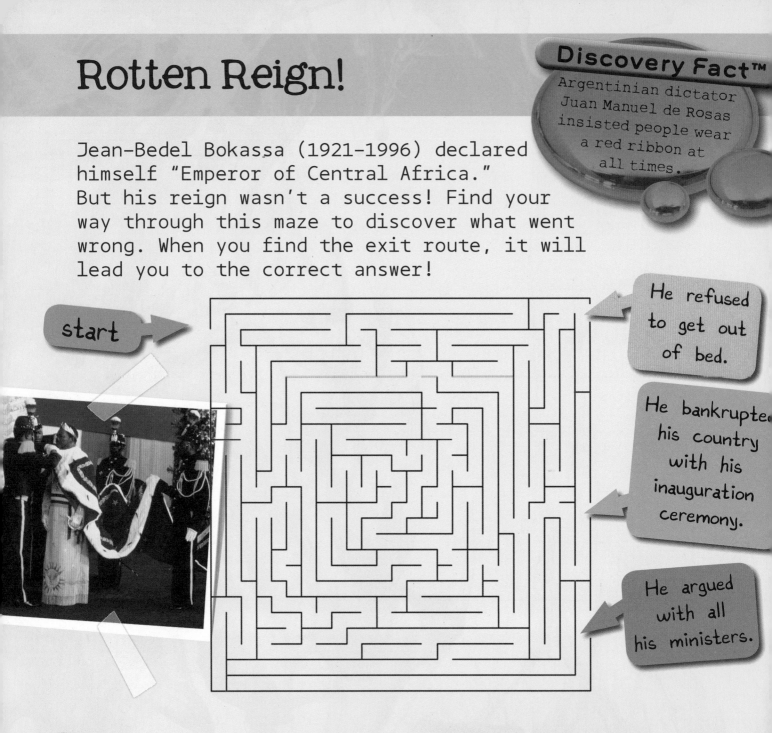

He refused to get out of bed.

He bankrupted his country with his inauguration ceremony.

He argued with all his ministers.

10

Crafty Creative!

When famous playwright William Shakespeare couldn't find the right word, he just invented it. Unscramble the letters below to discover some of the words he invented.

Ⓐ **yanz**

_ _ _ _

Ⓑ **nmeoobam**

_ _ _ _ _ _ _ _

Ⓒ **oerttur**

_ _ _ _ _ _ _

How Many Words?

Now solve the numbers to find out just how many words William Shakespeare invented!

$$1{,}000 + 500 + 200 = \boxed{}$$

Answer: [   ] words

Shakespeare lived from 1564 to 1616. Many people think he was the greatest playwright ever.

Colorful Composers!

Ludwig van Beethoven (1770–1827; pictured below) is one of the most famous composers of all time, but he was an odd character. Answer the questions in the crossword puzzle, then read down the gray box to reveal which part of his body he used to dip in water before he composed.

				1.				
2.								
		3.						
				4.				

1. The part of your body you use to play a piano keyboard.

2. A long, thin instrument you hold sideways and play with your mouth and fingers.

3. An instrument with black and white keys.

4. A loud instrument you beat with sticks.

Answer: 1. Hands, 2. Flute, 3. Piano, 4. Drum. Main answer: Head

Is It Art?

Many artists are noted for their odd behavior. Follow the lines to match each of these artists with their peculiarity.

A. Had an intense fear of grasshoppers.

B. Chopped off his own ear.

C. Painted pictures on the floor.

1. Whistler

2. van Gogh

3. Salvador Dali (pictured)

Discovery Fact™

When he was asked what he did with his old clothes, shabby artist L.S. Lowry replied, "I wear them!"

Outside the Law!

Legend has it that an outlaw lived in Sherwood Forest, England, in the 1300s, and robbed from the rich to give to the poor. Crack the code to discover his name.

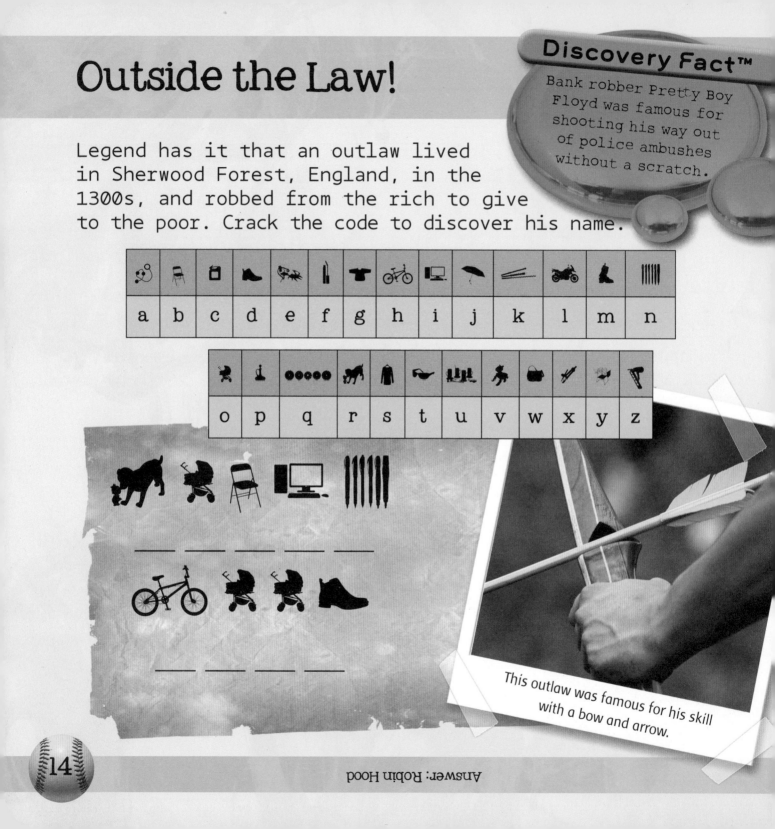													
a	b	c	d	e	f	g	h	i	j	k	l	m	n

o	p	q	r	s	t	u	v	w	x	y	z

___ ___ ___ ___ ___

___ ___ ___ ___

This outlaw was famous for his skill with a bow and arrow.

Answer: Robin Hood

Smooth Criminal!

Read around the word circles to discover the name of the man who masterminded the Great Train Robbery of 1963 in England. The first letter of each word is the letter in the center of the circle.

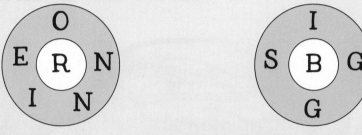

__ __ __ __ __ __ __ __   __ __ __ __ __

Highway Robbery!

In England in the 1700s and 1800s, robbers on horseback, known as highwaymen, attacked coaches on the road. Do the math below to discover how many miles famous highwayman Nick Nevison rode on horseback in just 14 hours to provide himself with an alibi.

$$(50 \times 2) + 10 + 90 = \boxed{}$$

Answer: $\boxed{}$ miles

Stinking Rich!

French King Louis XIV (1638–1715) once built something that cost a staggering one Fourth of France's annual income! Read clockwise around the word squares, starting from any letter, to discover what it was, then fill in the answer in the spaces below.

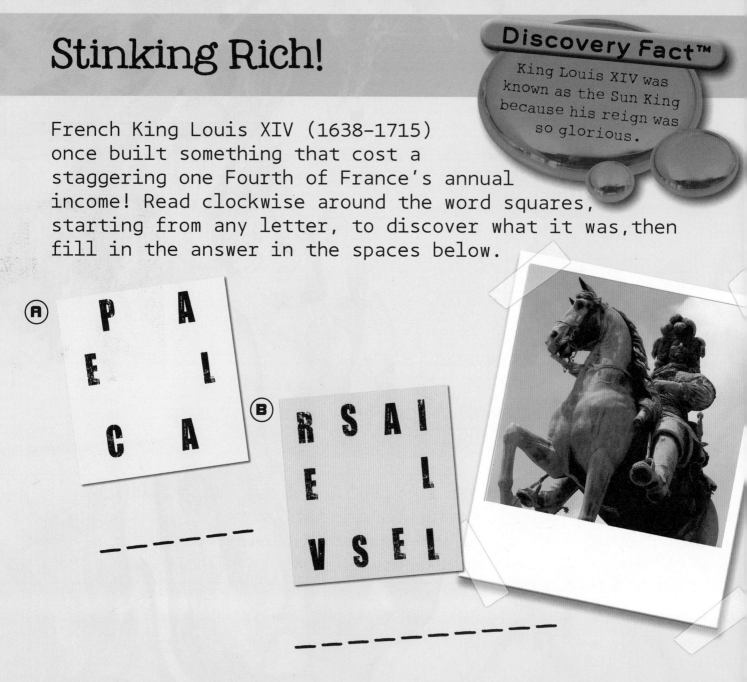

(A)

P A
P   A
E   L
  A
C A

(B)

R S A I
R   I
E   L
V S E L

He built the _ _ _ _ _ _ (A) of _ _ _ _ _ _ _ _ _ _ (B)

Answer: He built the Palace of Versailles. (It's just outside Paris, France, and you can still visit it today.)

Want a Cup of Coffee?

Believe it or not, some people are willing to pay $50 for a cup of Indonesian Kopi Luwak coffee. But what makes it so special? Work your way through the maze to find out. When you find the exit route, it will lead you to the correct answer.

start

The beans are covered in gold leaf.

The beans are grown in only one small village in Indonesia.

Weasel-like palm civets eat the beans, then poop them out.

Answer: Weasel-like palm civets eat the beans, then poop them out.

How Much?

We all know cars can cost a fortune, but just how many hard-earned bucks are some individuals willing to pay to buy this Bentley? Do the math to find out.

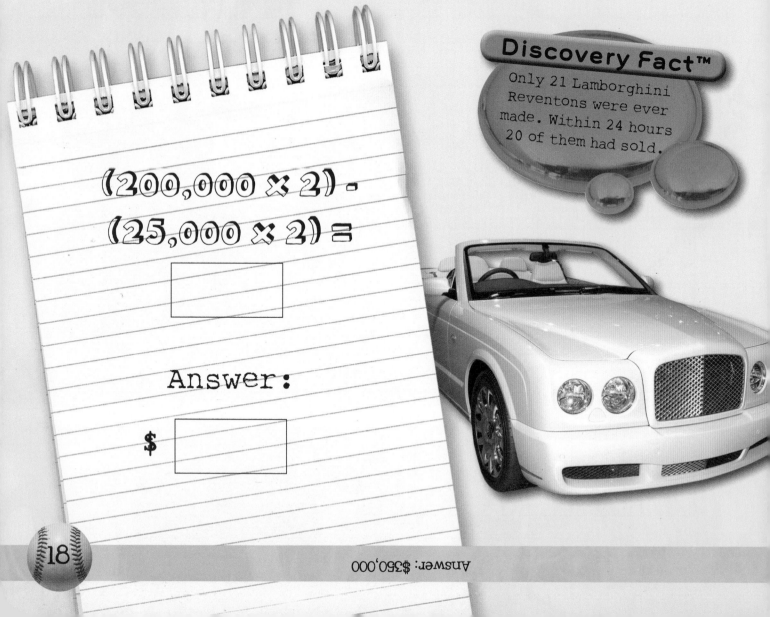

Discovery Fact™

Only 21 Lamborghini Reventons were ever made. Within 24 hours 20 of them had sold.

$$(200,000 \times 2) -$$
$$(25,000 \times 2) =$$

Answer:

$

Mad Money!

Having oodles of cash can make you lose touch with reality. Eccentric billionaire Howard Hughes had so much money he thought nothing of paying for a room in a luxurious hotel for a special guest. But who was the guest? Crack the code to find out!

a	b	c	d	e	f	g	h	i	j	k	l	m	n

o	p	q	r	s	t	u	v	w	x	y	z

_ _ _ _ _ _

_ _ _

Discovery Fact™

When he ate cake, Hughes insisted it be cut up into perfect squares, measured with a ruler!

Answer: A stray cat

Flash the Cash!

Someone, somewhere, is walking with these blinged-out accessories on them. Follow the lines to match each one with the correct price tag.

A. Platinum-body, diamond-encrusted Diamond Crypto Smartphone

B. Diamond-encrusted Chopard watch

C. Diamond-encrusted, gold-plated TrekStor MP3 player

1. $24 million

2. $1.3 million

3. $26,000

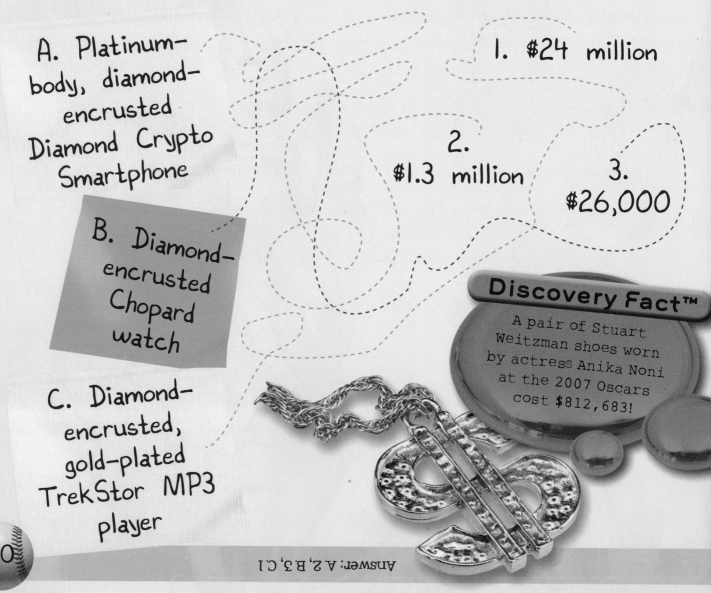

Discovery Fact™

A pair of Stuart Weitzman shoes worn by actress Anika Noni at the 2007 Oscars cost $812,683!

Answer: A.2, B.3, C.1

Deadly Dracula!

Discovery Fact™

The character Count Dracula was invented by author Bram Stoker in 1897.

The character Count Dracula was inspired by a real-life tyrant who lived in Bran Castle (pictured), Transylvania, in the 1400s. But what was his real name? Read around the word circles to find out. The first letter of each word is the letter in the center of the circle.

Ⓐ
L V A D

Ⓑ
P M I A R P I E L

(A) _ _ _ _ the

(B) _ _ _ _ _ _ _ _

21

Space Mission!

When an explosion disabled Apollo 13 as it neared the Moon in 1970, its crew overcame crippling cold, low oxygen, and lack of water to return to Earth safely. But what caused the explosion in the first place? Crack the code to find out!

z	y	x	w	v	u	t	s	r	q	p	o	n	m	l	k	j	i	h	g	f	e	d	c	b	a
a	b	c	d	e	f	g	h	i	j	k	l	m	n	o	p	q	r	s	t	u	v	w	x	y	z

g	s	v		l	c	b	t	v	m		g	z	m	p

v	c	k	o	l	w	v	w

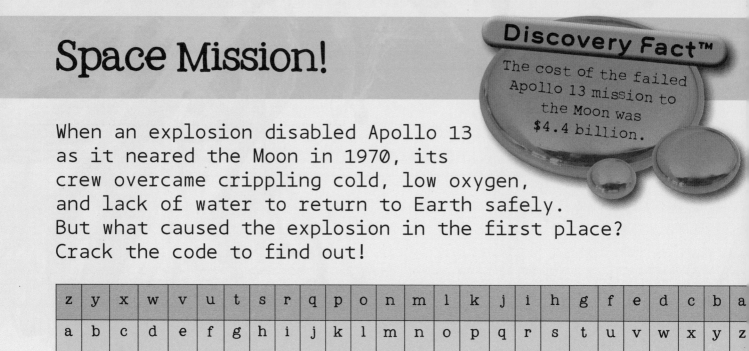

The three crew members were James A. Lovell, John L. Swigert, and Fred W. Haise.

22

Desert Island!

The famous story of Robinson Crusoe was inspired by a British sailor who survived four years on a desert island, until he was picked up in 1709. Work your way through the maze to find the name of the sailor. When you find the exit route, it will lead you to the correct answer!

start

LongJohn Silver

Alexander Selkirk

Captain William Bligh

Answer: Alexander Selkirk

True Survivors!

Do the math below to discover how many days Vietnamese fisherman Bui Duc Phuc survived at sea in 2004.

$$40 - 20 - 7 + 1 = \boxed{}$$

Answer: $\boxed{}$ days

Turn on the Light!

Inventor Thomas Edison was afraid of the dark, which may have encouraged him to come up with one of his most famous inventions. What was it? Unscramble the letters below to find out.

HTE GLIHTLUBB

___ _____

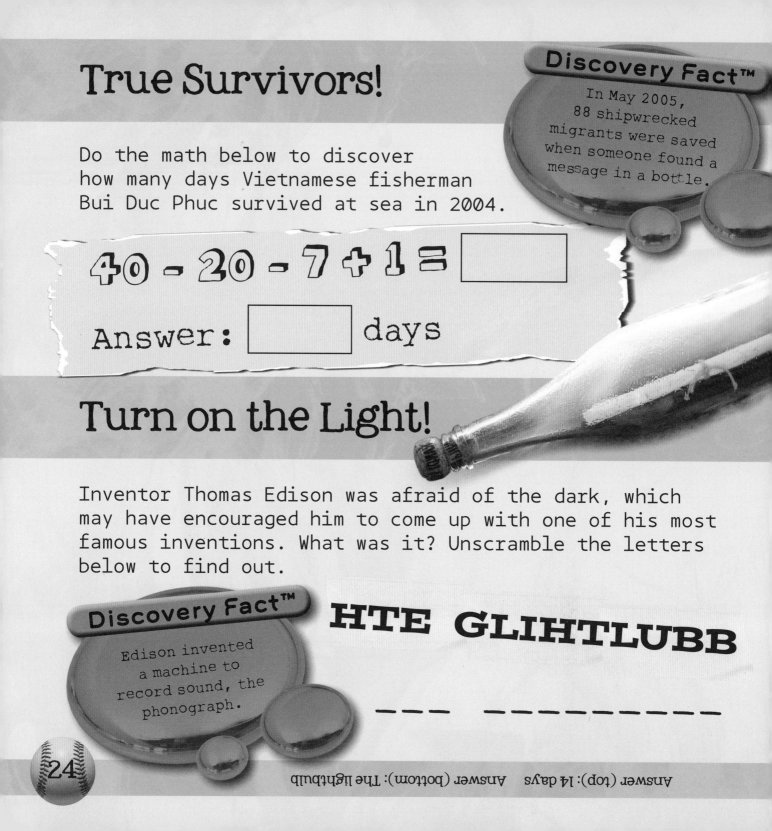

24

Brain Box!

Leonardo da Vinci (1452–1519) was so far ahead of his time, he created designs for all kinds of modern inventions! Answer the questions in the crossword puzzle, then read down the gray box to reveal the name of one.

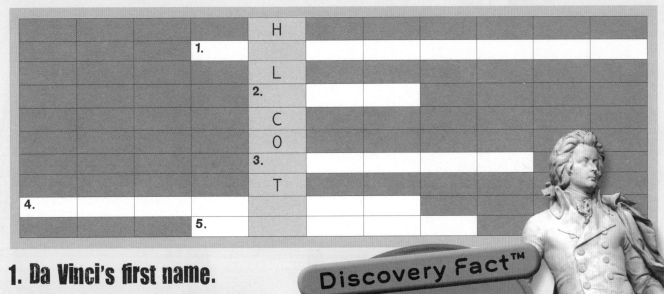

1. Da Vinci's first name.

2. The colored liquid in a pen.

3. The pages of a book are made from this.

4. The place where works of art are displayed.

5. You use it to put paint on a picture.

Discovery Fact™

After hearing Allegri's work Miserere just once, Mozart (pictured) remembered every note.

Answer: 1. Leonardo, 2. Ink, 3. Paper, 4. Gallery, 5. Brush.
Main answer: Helicopter

I've Got a Headache!

Doctors in the ancient world had some very strange ideas, and came up with some wacky and dangerous treatments. Follow the lines to match each ancient treatment to the right illness. Don't try any of these at home!

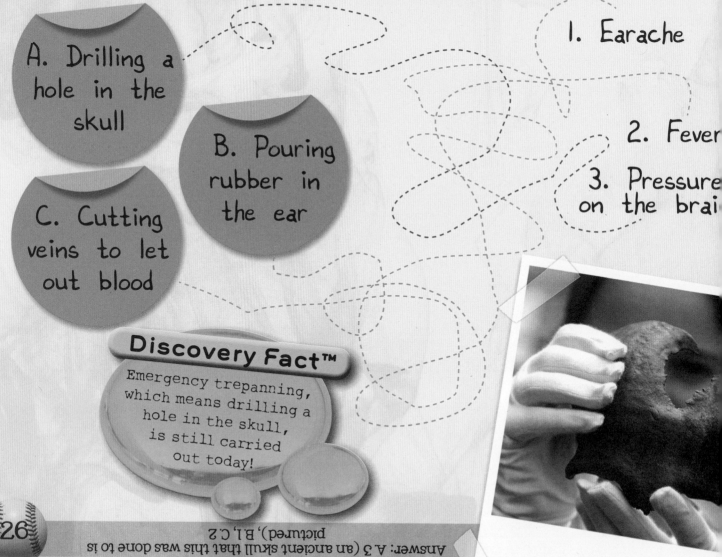

A. Drilling a hole in the skull

B. Pouring rubber in the ear

C. Cutting veins to let out blood

1. Earache

2. Fever

3. Pressure on the brain

Discovery Fact™

Emergency trepanning, which means drilling a hole in the skull, is still carried out today!

Answer: A 3 (an ancient skull that this was done to is pictured), B 1, C 2

I Can't See!

Discovery Fact™

The ancient Egyptians replaced missing toes with wooden ones!

If you were old and losing your vision, the ancient Egyptians had a handy remedy. To find out what, work your way through the maze. When you find the exit route, it will lead you to the correct answer.

Wear a blindfold soaked in urine.

Shave your eyebrows.

Rub your eyes with mashed tortoise brains and honey.

start

27

I Need a Doctor!

How good is your ancient medical knowledge? Let's find out! Try using this code buster to crack the answers to the questions below.

z	y	x	w	v	u	t	s	r	q	p	o	n	m	l	k	j	i	h	g	f	e	d	c	b	a
a	b	c	d	e	f	g	h	i	j	k	l	m	n	o	p	q	r	s	t	u	v	w	x	y	z

A What did Stone Age people use to stitch up wounds?

y	l	m	v		m	v	v	w	o	v	h

z	m	w		h	r	m	v	d		g	s	i	v	z	w	h

B According to their Code of Hammurabi, what did an ancient Assyrian doctor have to do if one of their patients died?

x	s	l	k		l	u	u		g	s	v	r	i		s	z	m	w

Answer: A. Bone needles and sinew threads. B. Chop off their hand.

Quacks and Quirks!

In the 1880s, Dr. Samuel Thomson gave sick people hot steam baths, cayenne pepper, and then made them vomit with a final ingredient. What was it? Read clockwise around the squares, starting from any letter, to find out what it is.

l o b
a e
i l
o w e
l
f s r

A Moving Story!

Dr. John Harvey Kellogg treated patients with a continual flow of water from both ends. Do the math below to discover how many gallons of water he could swish through a patient's body in just a few seconds.

$$(2 \times 5) + 10 - 4 = \boxed{}$$

Answer: $\boxed{}$ gallons

Discovery Fact™

Dr. Kellogg was also the inventor of cornflakes!

29

Cutting-Edge Surgery!

In the days before anesthetics, surgeons had to operate with little more than a saw and a bottle of whiskey (for the patient!). So what was the one quality that all patients looked for in their surgeon? Unscramble the letters below to find the answer.

Ⓐ **DEEPS** _ _ _ _ _

And unscramble these letters to find out what was the nickname given to surgeons in the old days.

Ⓑ **WASNBOES** _ _ _ _ _ _ _ _

Major Surgery!

Jean-Baptiste Denys carried out the first (unsuccessful!) blood transfusion in the 1800s. What kind of blood did he use? Read around the word circle to find out! The first letter of the word is the letter in the center of the circle.

_ _ _ _ _

Answer (bottom): Lamb's   Answer (top): A. Speed, B. Sawbones

You're Pulling My Leg!

In the fourth century A.D., saints Cosmas and Damian are said to have given a priest a transplant to save him from blood poisoning. Answer the questions in the crossword puzzle, then read down the gray box to discover which body part they transplanted.

1. The sharp part of a knife, used for cutting.

2. This is given to patients to put them to sleep for an operation.

3. The name for a doctor who does operations.

Discovery Fact™

The first amputation done under anesthesia was carried out in London, England, in 1847.

31

It's Hair Raising!

In the olden days, surgeons had no medical training. In fact, they often had another job, too. Work your way through the maze to find out what it was. When you find the exit route, it will lead you to the correct answer.

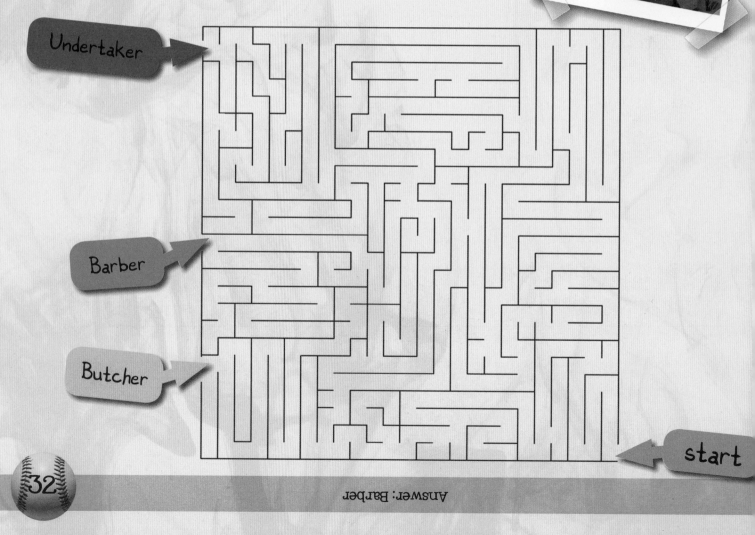

Undertaker

Barber

Butcher

start

Deadly Plague!

Discovery Fact™

Doctors visiting plague victims wore a metal beak stuffed with herbs, a leather gown, and gloves.

People have had some pretty strange ideas about how illnesses spread in the past. How did the people believe the Black Death—a terrifying plague that swept Europe between 1347 and 1351—was spread?

a	b	c	d	e	f	g	h	i	j	k	l	m	n

o	p	q	r	s	t	u	v	w	x	y	z

A They thought it was spread by

— — — — — — — — — —

B How was the disease really spread?

— — — — — — — — —

33

The Great Plague of London!

The huge wave of plague that hit London, England, between 1665 and 1666 was one of the most devastating ever. Do the math below to discover how many people died.

$$(50 \times 2) + (25 \times 4) - (50 \times 2) = \boxed{}$$

Answer: $\boxed{}$ thousand

What Percentage?

Now do the math to find out what percentage of London's population died.

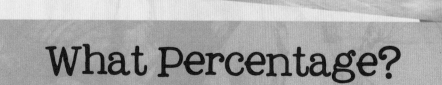

$$2 + 15 + 1 + 2 = \boxed{}$$

Answer: $\boxed{}$ percent

34

Are You Crazy?

With all those killer diseases out there, you'd think that people would take better care of their health, but many don't. Two out of three people in rich countries die younger than they should because they eat too much of the wrong kinds of food. What are these foods? Read around the word circles to find out! The first letter of each word is the letter in the center of the circle.

In Sickness and in Health

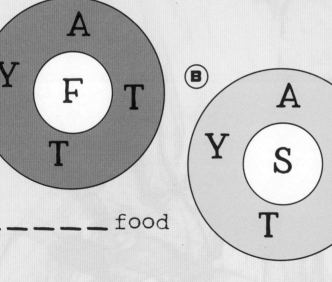

A

A
Y F T
T

_ _ _ _ _ _ food

B

A
Y S L
T

_ _ _ _ _ _ food

C

G
U S A
Y R

_ _ _ _ _ _ _ food

It's Catching!

Throughout history, people have had all kinds of odd ideas about how diseases are spread—evil spirits, bad smells, even curses. Follow the lines to find out how the diseases below are really spread.

A.
Bites from infected mosquitoes

B.
By coughing and sneezing

C.
By drinking dirty water

1. Cholera

2. Measles

3. Malaria

Answer: A3, B2, C1

Name that Disease!

Brainy scientists have a habit of giving diseases long, complicated names that are hard to pronounce—so we shorten the names to make them easier to remember. Do you know the full names of these three diseases? Use the code buster to find the answers.

z	y	x	w	v	u	t	s	r	q	p	o	n	m	l	k	j	i	h	g	f	e	d	c	b	a
a	b	c	d	e	f	g	h	i	j	k	l	m	n	o	p	q	r	s	t	u	v	w	x	y	z

(A) TB

g	f	y	v	i	x	f	o	l	h	r	h

(B) AIDS

z	x	j	f	r	i	v	w	r	n	n	f	m	l	w	v	u	r	x	r	v	m	x	b

(C) MS

h	b	m	w	i	l	n	v

n	f	o	g	r	k	o	v	h	x	o	v	i	l	h	r	h

Answer: 1. Tuberculosis, 2. Acquired immunodeficiency syndrome, 3. Multiple sclerosis

Malaria!

Over 300 million people get malaria each year, but numbers could be reduced if we made sure everyone in infected areas had a mosquito net. But we don't. Crazy, huh? Answer the questions in the crossword puzzle, then read down the gray box to discover what "malaria" means.

1. A red substance that is pumped around your body.

2. The organ that pumps blood around your body.

3. The deadly plague that swept Europe between 1347 and 1351.

4. A disease spread by mosquitoes.

5. A smelly habit that can cause lung cancer.

6. Small rodents covered in fleas.

Answer: 1. Blood, 2. Heart, 3. Black Death, 4. Malaria, 5. Smoking, 6. Rats.
Main answer: Bad air

Ghastly Germs!

You'd be crazy to be lazy when it comes to cleanliness! The microscopic germs that cause disease are everywhere. There are three main kinds, each causing different diseases. Follow the lines to match each kind with an illness it causes.

1. Flu

2. Malaria

3. The plague

A. Bacteria

B. Viruses

C. Protozoa

Discovery Fact™

Not all bacteria are bad. Many live harmlessly in your bowels.

Achoo!

Everyone's nose runs, but do you know just how fast your nose really is? When you have a cold and sneeze, snot shoots out at hundreds of miles an hour. But how many viruses are there in just one sneeze? Work your way through the maze to find out. When you find the exit route, it will lead you to the correct answer.

start

100 thousan...

One million

6 million

Answer: 6 million

Your Awesome Body!

There are billions of microscopic nasties out there that can make you sick, but your body is equipped with an awesome defense system to help you fight them off. Do the math to find how many billion viruses there can be in a single drop of blood!

10 - 6 + 3 - 2 =

Answer: ____ billion

This magnified picture shows what viruses look like.

A Moving Story!

Now do the math to find out how many thousands of bacteria would fit across your fingernail if they lined up in single file.

20 + 10 - 20 =

Answer: ____ thousand

Pass Me a Tissue!

Your body might have an awesome defense system, but it can still catch about 250 versions of one common illness. Read clockwise around the squares, starting from any letter, to find out what it is.

C O M

N O M

_ _ _ _ _ _ _

D C

L O

_ _ _ _

Rotten Rashes!

Discovery Fact™

Ringworm is not a worm at all, but a fungus that grows on the skin.

Your skin can break out in nasty pimples and rashes—but they often look more serious than they are. Can you match these common lumps and bumps with their cause?

A. A ring-shaped rash.

B. Pus-filled pimples on the face.

C. Tiny cauliflower-shape lumps on the hands and feet.

1. Ringworm

2. Warts

3. Acne

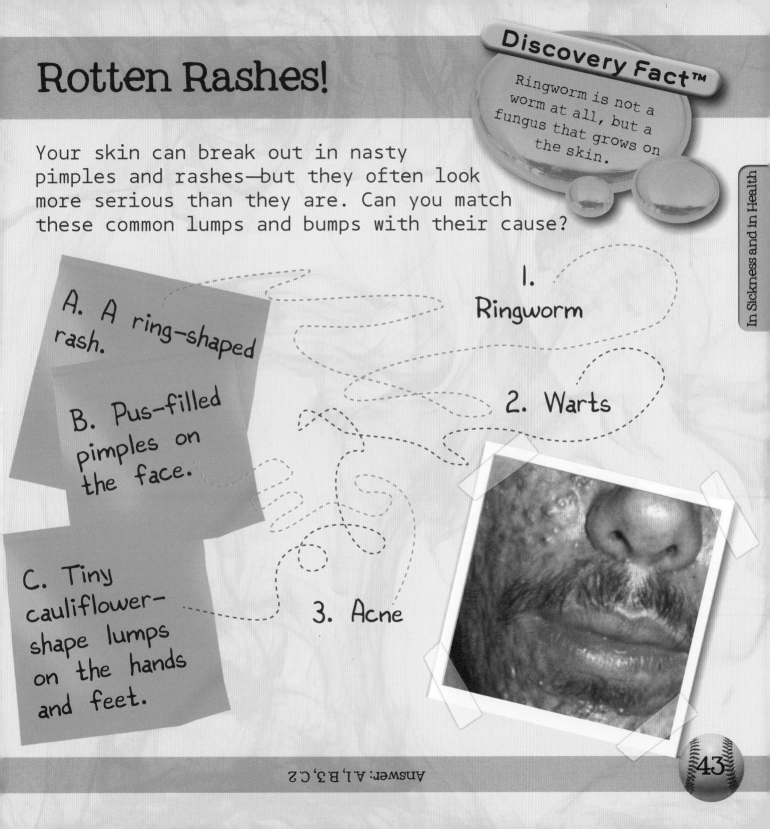

Answer: A.1, B.3, C.2

Miraculous Medicine!

Spending your time looking at dishes of mold might sound a little crazy, but for scientist Alexander Fleming it led to a medical discovery of momentous proportions. What was it? Crack the code below to find out.

z	y	x	w	v	u	t	s	r	q	p	o	n	m	l	k	j	i	h	g	f	e	d	c	b	a
a	b	c	d	e	f	g	h	i	j	k	l	m	n	o	p	q	r	s	t	u	v	w	x	y	z

k	v	m	r	x	r	o	o	r	m

g	s	v		u	r	i	h	g		z	m	g	r	y	r	l	g	r	x

Discovery Fact™

Aspirin is based on a natural chemical found in willow bark.

44

Smooth Operators!

Surgery has come a long way since the invention of anesthetics 150 years ago. Soon, we might not even need surgeons at all. But who or what would perform operations instead? Answer the questions in the crossword puzzle, then read down the gray box to discover the answer.

1. A sweet food you shouldn't eat too much of.

2. The most common illness.

3. Is plague caused by bacteria or a virus?

4. Someone who treats you when you are ill.

5. What kind of medicine is penicillin?

6. Is flu caused by bacteria or a virus?

Answer: 1. Sugar, 2. Cold, 3. Bacteria, 4. Doctor, 5. Antibiotic, 6. Virus. Main answer: Robots.

Crazy Cavemen!

Early humans liked to create cave paintings using dirt or charcoal. But what did they mix it with? To find out, work your way through the maze. When you find the exit route, it will lead you to the correct answer.

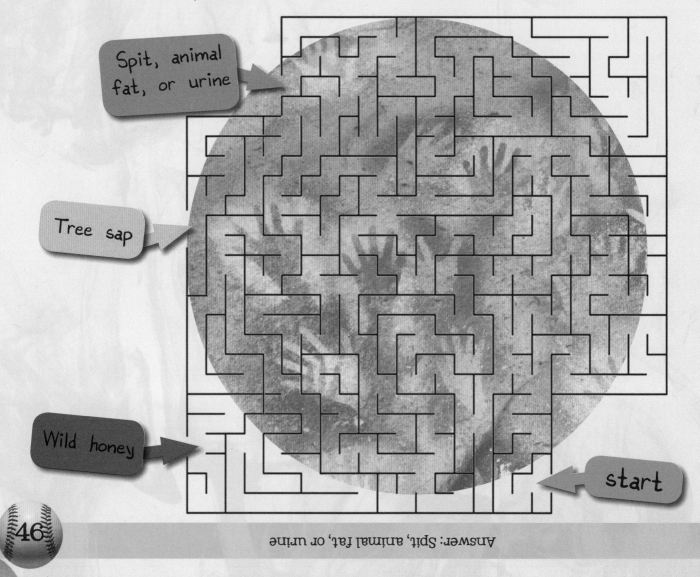

Murder Mystery!

Tollund Man, a 2,000-year-old murder victim, was discovered in a peat bog in Denmark in 1950. How did he die? To solve the mystery, unscramble the letters below.

He was **GEDHAN**

_ _ _ _ _ _

by a **PROE**

_ _ _ _

Discovery Fact™

Tollund Man's last meal was still in his stomach: vegetable porridge and a type of fungus that would have given him hallucinations.

Awesome Ancestors

Icky Evolution!

Discovery Fact™

Modern humans first appeared around 200,000 years ago.

Human civilization has come a very long way since modern humans first walked the Earth. But who do you think were probably our VERY first ancestors? Find your way through this maze to find out. When you find the exit route, it will lead you to the correct answer!

start

Dinosaurs

Hairy apelike creatures

Slimy sea creatures

Answer: Slimy sea creatures. (We are also descended from hairy apelike creatures, but the sea creatures came first!)

Going Public!

To find out just how "public" Roman bathrooms really were, decode these word squares to find the hidden words, then write them in the spaces below. Read clockwise around each square, starting from any letter, to find the answers.

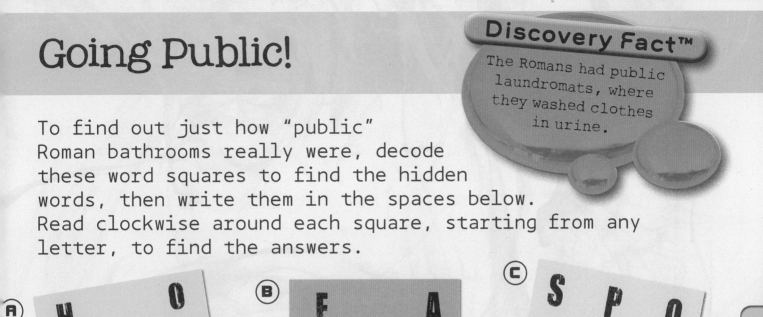

Ⓐ
H O
S L
E

Ⓑ
E A
S T

Ⓒ
S P O
E G N

Roman public toilets were a line of
(A)_ _ _ _ _ in a long (B)_ _ _ _, set over running water. People wiped themselves with a _ _ _ _ _ _ (C) on a stick, which they shared!

Awesome Ancestors

Answer: Roman public toilets were a line of holes in a long seat, set over running water. People wiped themselves with a sponge on a stick, which they shared!

A Disgusting Day Out!

The Romans loved nothing better than watching gladiators fight to the death. Where did these bloodthirsty games take place in ancient Rome? Answer the questions in the crossword puzzle, then read down the gray box to find out.

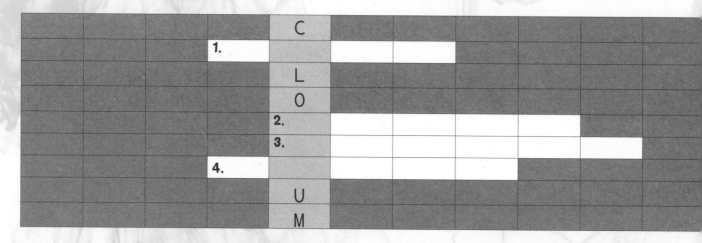

1. The capital of Italy.

2. A weapon with a long, sharp blade.

3. A large metal, platelike object, used to protect yourself in battle.

4. Gladiators often fought to the _ _ _ _ _.

Answer: 1. Rome, 2. Sword, 3. Shield, 4. Death. Main answer: Colosseum (pictured)

Banquet Time!

Noble Romans were famous for holding enormous banquets and stuffing their faces with enormous quantities of food. What was the "polite" response to show you had enjoyed your meal?

start

A round of applause

A long speech

A big burp!

Awesome Ancestors

Answer: A big burp!

Oh Mummy!

The ancient Egyptians were experts at preserving dead bodies as mummies. Some of the equipment they used to carry out this task is hidden in these circles. Can you decode them? The first letter of each word is the letter in the center of the circle.

A)
A
T **S** L

_ _ _ _ _

B)
A
M **H** R
E
M

_ _ _ _ _ _

C)
H
I **C** L
S
E

_ _ _ _ _ _

D)
P
N **S** O
O

_ _ _ _ _

E)
S A
E **B** N
G D
A

_ _ _ _ _ _ _

Answer: A. Salt, B. Hammer, C. Chisel, D. Spoon, E. Bandages

Hiding a Fortune!

Many ancient Egyptian kings and queens (called pharaohs) were buried in tombs inside huge pyramids, along with everything they could possibly need in the afterlife, including treasure! How did the builders scare away grave robbers? Crack the code to find out.

z	y	x	w	v	u	t	s	r	q	p	o	n	m	l	k	j	i	h	g	f	e	d	c	b	a
a	b	c	d	e	f	g	h	i	j	k	l	m	n	o	p	q	r	s	t	u	v	w	x	y	z

x	f	i	h	v	h		l	m		g	s	v		d	z	o	o	h

Discovery Fact™

A gold mask of Pharaoh Tutankhamun's face was discovered in his tomb by archeologists.

Answer: Curses on the walls

The Golden Age!

The most famous pirate captains sailed the seas off the America's during a time called the "Golden Age." But when was this? Do the math below to find out.

2,000 - 200 - 100 = ☐

Answer: The ☐ s

Pirates Ahoy!

Pirate flags were designed to scare people! Read around the two word circles to discover the name for these flags. Each word starts with the letter in the center of the circle.

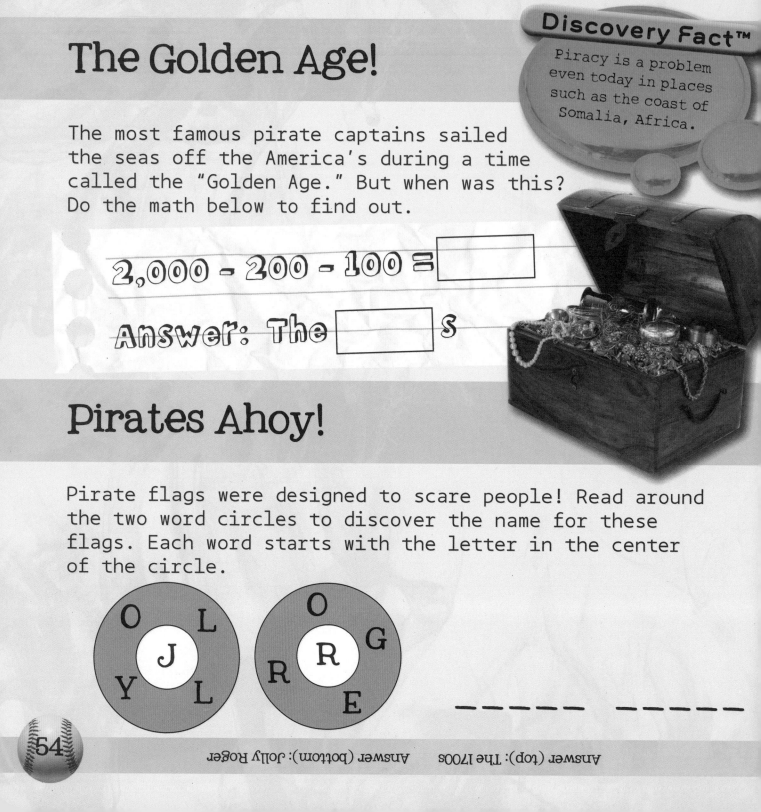

O L J Y L

O R G R E

_ _ _ _ _   _ _ _ _ _

Answer (bottom): Jolly Roger   Answer (top): The 1700s

Let's Party!

Pirates had hideouts where they could blow their stolen loot and party the night away. The name of one pirate island in the Caribbean is hidden in this word square. Can you work it out? Read clockwise around the square, starting from any letter.

```
U G A
    T
T R O
```

- - - - - - - - -

Discovery Fact™

Many pirates actually tried to capture the enemy without a battle, usually by scaring them into surrender!

Under Attack!

Soldiers attacking a medieval castle used some mean missiles, including flaming arrows, rocks, and even rotting dead animals, fired by a weapon known as the trebuchet. Work your way through the maze to find out what a trebuchet is.

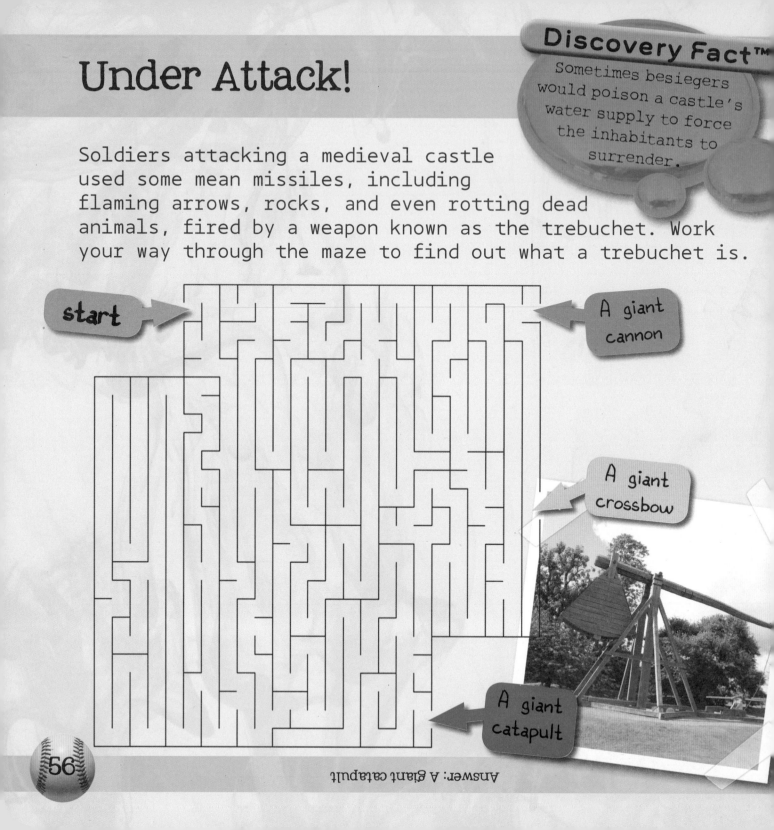

start

A giant cannon

A giant crossbow

A giant catapult

Answer: A giant catapult

Phew!

In 1203, some enterprising French knights sneaked their way inside a besieged castle in a unique, if unpleasant, way. To find out how they got in, crack the code below!

z	y	x	w	v	u	t	s	r	q	p	o	n	m	l	k	j	i	h	g	f	e	d	c	b	a
a	b	c	d	e	f	g	h	i	j	k	l	m	n	o	p	q	r	s	t	u	v	w	x	y	z

They crawled
through the castle's

h	v	d	z	t	v		g	i	v	m	x	s

Medieval castles were often surrounded by a ditch of water, called a moat, to protect them from attackers.

Discovery Fact™

Boys started to train to be knights when they were about eight years old.

Answer: They crawled through the castle's sewage trench.

It's a Knockout!

Discovery Fact™

Knights often had to have limbs amputated.

Believe it or not, knights of old were very fond of a dangerous sport that involved knocking your opponent off their horse with a big, long stick! Crack the code below to discover the name of this sport.

a	b	c	d	e	f	g	h	i	j	k	l	m	n

o	p	q	r	s	t	u	v	w	x	y	z

_ _ _ _ _ _ _ _

Answer: Jousting

Surprise Disguise!

When hunting bison as they roamed the prairie, how do you think Native Americans disguised themselves? Crack the code to find the answer!

z	y	x	w	v	u	t	s	r	q	p	o	n	m	l	k	j	i	h	g	f	e	d	c	b	a
a	b	c	d	e	f	g	h	i	j	k	l	m	n	o	p	q	r	s	t	u	v	w	x	y	z

They crawled on the ground dressed in

d	l	o	u		h	p	r	m	h

Wolves hunt in packs. A pack can successfully bring down large animals, such as bison and deer.

Discovery Fact™

Native Americans admired wolves and their hunting skills.

Answer: Wolf skins

Have a Sip!

Medieval medical men thought they could tell a lot from a patient's urine. Sometimes they examined it when it was fresh and warm by smelling it, but they also tested it in a weirder way, too! Answer the questions in the crossword puzzle, then read down the gray box to find out how!

			1.									
		2.										
					3.							
					4.							
			5.									

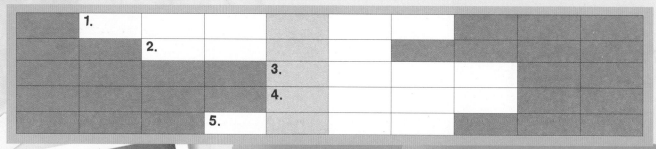

1. Someone who treats you when you are ill.

2. Something you use to wash your hands.

3. Another word for "ill."

4. You have five of these on each foot.

5. The part of your body housing your brain.

Discovery Fact™

In times of old, artists used urine to mix pigments to make their paint.

Answer: 1. Doctor, 2. Soap, 3. Sick, 4. Toes, 5. Head. Main answer: Taste

It's All About Style!

Fashion throughout history has often made people look totally foolish. In the 1100s, stylish individuals wouldn't be seen dead on the street without a pair of pikases. But what were they? Crack the code to find out.

z	y	x	w	v	u	t	s	r	q	p	o	n	m	l	k	j	i	h	g	f	e	d	c	b	a
a	b	c	d	e	f	g	h	i	j	k	l	m	n	o	p	q	r	s	t	u	v	w	x	y	z

h	s	l	v	h		d	r	g	s		o	l	m	t		x	f	i	o	b		g	l	v	h

Answer: Shoes with long curly toes

Skin Deep!

In the 1600s, fashionable men and women wore thick, white makeup-but they paid for their vanity. The makeup was so poisonous, it shriveled and rotted their skin. Read around the word circles to find the deadly ingredients in the mix. The first letter of each word is the letter in the center of the circle.

A

E T **W** H I

D A **L** E

_ _ _ _ _   _ _ _ _ _

B

E T **W** H I

I N **V** R A E G

_ _ _ _ _   _ _ _ _ _ _ _

Discovery Fact™

In the 1700s, wigs were sometimes made from real human hair collected from the poor, or dead people!

62

Breathtaking!

In the 1600s, men and women wore tight underwear reinforced with iron to make them look thinner. It's no wonder that the kings and queens often looked so grumpy in pictures! What was the name for these uncomfortable garments? Unscramble the letters to find out.

CROSSET

_ _ _ _ _ _ _

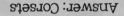
Answer: Corsets

Health Hazards!

The water people drank in Victorian London was so unhealthy that thousands of people caught diseases from it and died. Finally, the government decided to build something to solve the problem. Work your way through the maze to find out what it was. When you find the exit route, it will lead you to the correct answer!

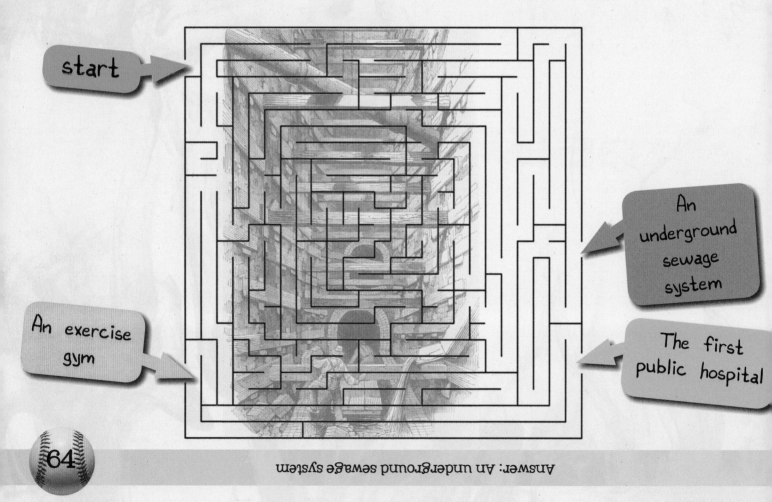

start

An underground sewage system

An exercise gym

The first public hospital

64

Answer: An underground sewage system

Lucky You!

Up until recent times, what was the normal way for teachers to discipline pupils who misbehaved? Work your way through the maze to find out. When you find the exit route, it will lead you to the correct answer!

start

Give them a detention

Politely ask them to behave

Hit them

$1 + 1 = 2$

Awesome Ancestors

The Worst School Ever?!

Around 500 BC, boys in Sparta, Greece, were sent away to military school to toughen them up. They had to sleep on beds of sharp reeds to get them used to pain, and lessons included staying silent while being whipped. Unscramble the letters below to discover how old these boys were.

VEENS SEYAR LOD

_ _ _ _ _

_ _ _ _ _   _ _ _

Discovery Fact™

Spartan girls competed in athletics to keep them fit, so that they would have healthy babies!

Answer: Seven years old

You Must Be Kidding!

For centuries, kids from poor families have had to work as soon as they could walk. It was especially bad in the 1800s, when a lot of new industries started up. Crack the code to discover two of the terrible jobs young children had to do.

z	y	x	w	v	u	t	s	r	q	p	o	n	m	l	k	j	i	h	g	f	e	d	c	b	a
a	b	c	d	e	f	g	h	i	j	k	l	m	n	o	p	q	r	s	t	u	v	w	x	y	z

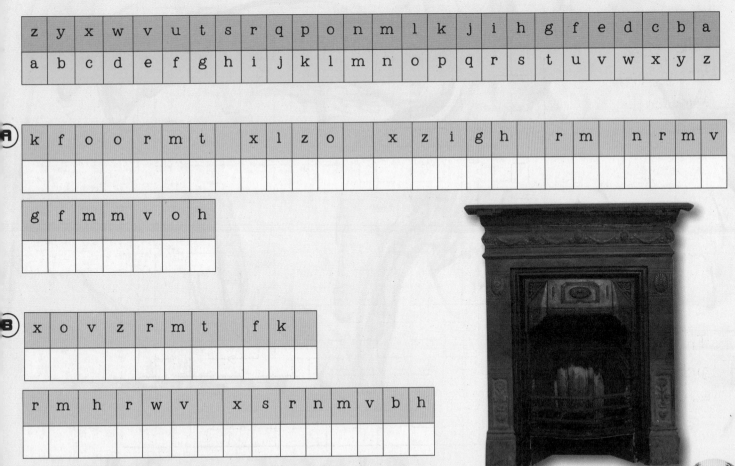

A)

k	f	o	o	r	m	t		x	l	z	o		x	z	i	g	h		r	m		n	r	m	v

g	f	m	m	v	o	h

B)

x	o	v	z	r	m	t		f	k

r	m	h	r	w	v		x	s	r	n	m	v	b	h

67

Tiny Feet!

In ancient China, it was considered very beautiful for girls to have tiny feet, so they attempted to restrict foot growth! Work your way through the maze to discover how they did this.

They bound the feet tightly with bandages.

They chopped off their toes.

They made girls wear very small shoes.

start

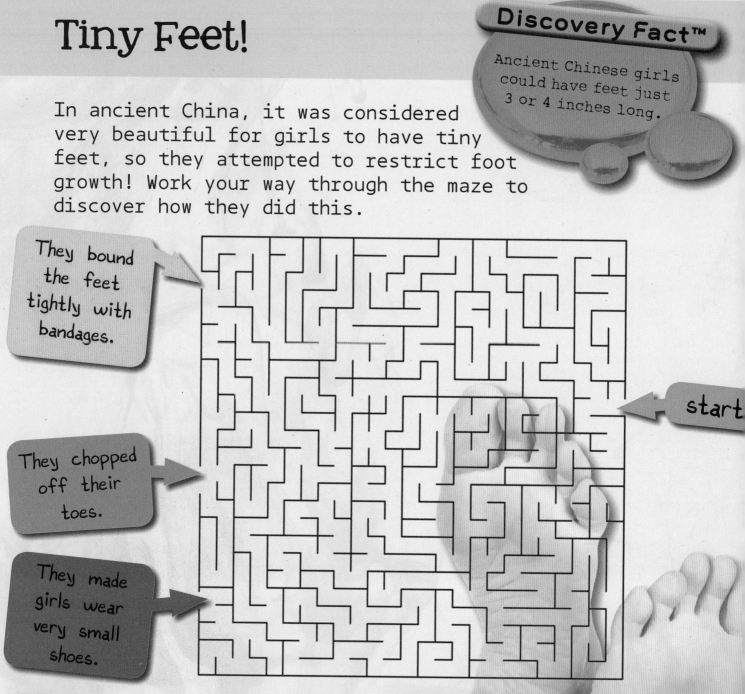

Answer: They bound the feet tightly with bandages (so that their feet didn't grow properly and stayed small).

It's Tradition!

In years gone by, many children died before they reached adulthood.

When you hear what some people did to their children, you'll be amazed that anyone survived. Can you match these cultures with their childcare?

1. Medieval Europe

2. Ancient China

3. Ancient Rome

A. Fathers could choose if a newborn baby should live or die.

B. Mothers fed babies food they had already chewed to make it mushy.

C. Babies were "swaddled," or wrapped, so tightly in bandages, they couldn't move (pictured).

Awesome Ancestors

Answer: A3, B1, C2

Yucky Science!

In 1683, microscope maker Antonie van Leeuwenhoek was the first person to observe bacteria from a human body. But which yucky gunk from his own body was he studying under a microscope when he spotted them? Unscramble the letters to find out.

Discovery Fact™

Antonie van Leeuwenhoek said he saw "many very little, living animalcules, very prettily a-moving."

HOOTT

_ _ _ _ _

QAPLUE

_ _ _ _ _ _

70

A Cut Above the Rest!

Why wouldn't you want to live next door to scientist Leonardo da Vinci, who lived in the 1400s? Work your way through the maze to find out. When you find the exit route, it will lead you to the correct answer!

He played loud music.

He threw wild parties.

He cut up dead horses and humans to see how they worked.

start

Freaky Scientists

Answer: He cut up dead horses and humans to see how they worked.

How Sick!

In 1796, English scientist Edward Jenner discovered how to protect people from the disease smallpox by injecting something rather revolting into a small boy. What was it? Answer the questions in the crossword puzzle, then read down the gray box to find out! Then write the word in the spaces below to finish the passage.

	1.					
	2.					
3.						

1. **You get covered with these if you catch the disease measles.**

2. **Someone who cares for the sick, but is not a doctor.**

3. **A place you go if you are very sick.**

He injected the boy with _ _ _ from a cowpox blister. The boy caught cowpox, which is a mild, harmless form of smallpox. Then Jenner injected him with _ _ _ from a smallpox blister to see if his theory that cowpox would protect him from smallpox was correct. Luckily it was!

This picture shows Jenner vaccinating his own son.

Answer: 1. Spots, 2. Nurse, 3. Hospital. Main answer: Pus

Mad Inventions!

History is littered with unsuccessful ideas by crazy inventors. Can you match these unsuccessful ideas with what went wrong?

A. Franz Reichelt invented a combined overcoat and parachute. He jumped off the Eiffel Tower in Paris (pictured).

B. Alexander Bogdanov thought blood transfusions could make people young again. He tested the idea on himself.

C. Thomas Midgley invented a pulley-operated mechanical bed.

1. It didn't open!

2. He accidentally strangled himself when testing it out.

3. He infected himself with deadly diseases.

Answer: A.1, B.3, C.2

Freaky Scientists

73

Rise and Shine!

The "Most Horrible Invention Award" must go to George Hogan. But what did he invent? Crack the code to find out.

z	y	x	w	v	u	t	s	r	q	p	o	n	m	l	k	j	i	h	g	f	e	d	c	b	a
a	b	c	d	e	f	g	h	i	j	k	l	m	n	o	p	q	r	s	t	u	v	w	x	y	z

z	m		z	o	z	i	n		x	o	l	x	p		g	s	z	g		g	r	k	h

x	l	o	w		d	z	g	v	i		w	l	d	m		b	l	f	i		m	v	x	p

Discovery Fact™

Scientists in Japan have invented a smell recorder that can "record" and "play back" smells.

Answer: An alarm clock that tips cold water down your neck.

Poop Science!

Scientists at the University of Washington receive poop through the mail from park rangers in Africa, and analyze it for DNA. This helps them create a poop-inspired map of one animal's population across Africa. Read around the word circle below to discover which animal.

E P
L H
E
T A
N

_ _ _ _ _ _ _ _ _

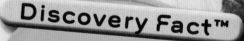

Discovery Fact™

DNA stands for deoxyribonucleic acid!

Answer: Elephant

Freaky Scientists

Rotten Science!

The smell of rotten food makes us gag, but there is a very good reason for this. The human body has evolved this way, to stop us from eating bad food and getting sick.

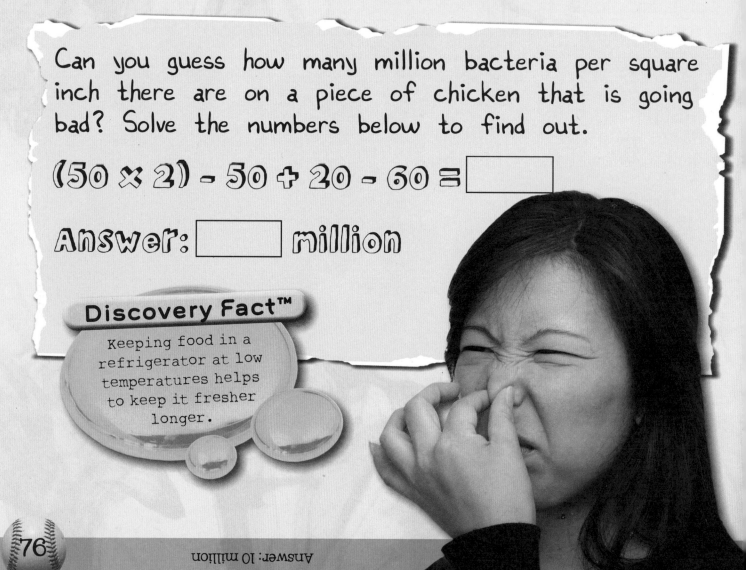

Can you guess how many million bacteria per square inch there are on a piece of chicken that is going bad? Solve the numbers below to find out.

$$(50 \times 2) - 50 + 20 - 60 = \boxed{}$$

Answer: $\boxed{}$ million

Discovery Fact™

Keeping food in a refrigerator at low temperatures helps to keep it fresher longer.

Strong Stomach!

There's nothing more amazing than the human body. For example, the acid in your stomach that kills off dangerous bacteria is highly corrosive, but, amazingly, a healthy stomach isn't harmed by it. To find out why not, unscramble the words below and finish the sentence.

Ⓐ CHASTOM

Ⓑ LYAER

The (A) _ _ _ _ _ _ _ is protected by a (B) _ _ _ _ _ of mucus.

Discovery Fact™

Not all bacteria are bad for you. Millions live harmlessly in your intestines.

Answer: The stomach is protected by a layer of mucus.

Freaky Scientists

Worst Smell?

Chemists have invented the world's worst smell—a mix of vomit, rotting flesh, and sweet fruit. The name of this stomach-churning recipe is hidden in these squares. Read clockwise around the squares, starting from any letter, to discover it!

S T E

H C N

_ _ _ _ _ _ _

P S

U O

_ _ _ _

Answer: Stench soup

Sounds a Bit Fishy!

Food scientists are always searching for ways to make food healthier, which is why Indian scientists developed an extra-healthy, low-fat ice cream. But what is their wacky secret ingredient? Find your way through the maze below to find out! When you find the exit route, it will lead you to the correct answer!

Sheep's milk

start

Sunflower oil

Cuttlefish

Freaky Scientists

Additives!

Food scientists add chemicals to food to alter its taste and make it last longer. This doesn't sound that crazy until you hear some of the other useful—but not so tasty—jobs these chemicals are used for. Can you match these food additives to their jobs?

A. A coloring in salad dressings, sun lotion, and paint.

B. Used in store-bought meals to stop ingredients from separating, and in soap.

C. Used in orange and lime-flavored foods, in beetle poison, deodorants, and to cool car engines.

1. Sodium phosphate

2. Propylene glycol

3. Titanium dioxide

Answer: A.3, B.1, C.2

Going Around in Circles!

Up until the early 1500s, everyone believed that the Sun traveled around the Earth—until one brave scientist dared to suggest it was the other way around. Answer the questions in the crossword puzzle, then read down the gray box to reveal his name.

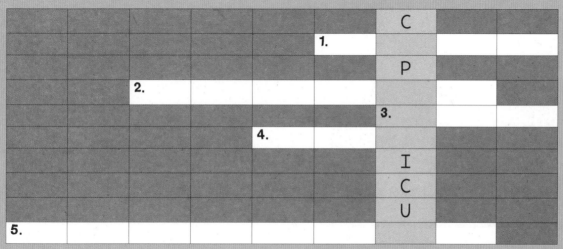

1. This rocky body travels around Earth.

2. A vehicle designed to travel in to space.

3. What color does Mars appear to be?

4. The star at the center of our solar system.

5. Which is bigger? The universe or a galaxy?

Answer: 1. Moon, 2. Rocket, 3. Red, 4. Sun, 5. Universe.
Main answer: Copernicus

Out of This World!

It's one thing to look at stars through a telescope, but what does it feel like to be in space? Russian astronaut Yuri Gagarin was the first person to find out. His successful mission on April 12, 1961, made him an international celebrity, but what was the name of his spacecraft? Read clockwise around the word square, starting from any letter, to find out.

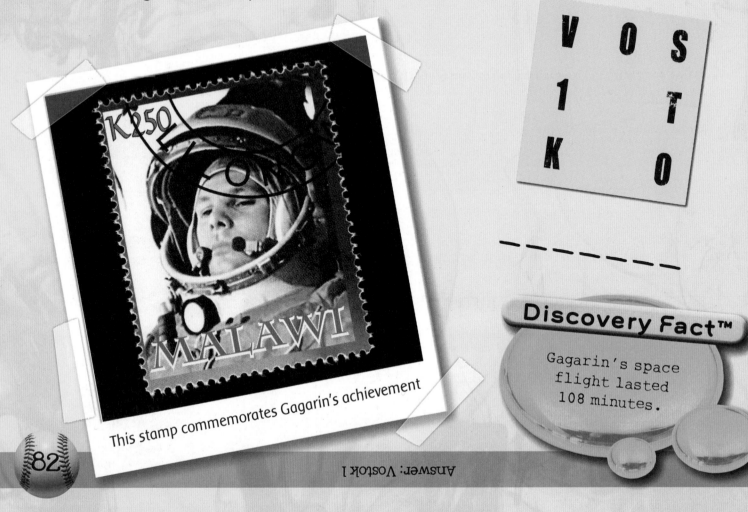

V O S
1   S
V   T
K   O

_ _ _ _ _ _ _

This stamp commemorates Gagarin's achievement

Discovery Fact™

Gagarin's space flight lasted 108 minutes.

Answer: Vostok 1

A Weighty Problem!

Scientists have figured out that you weigh less on Earth than on the bigger planets in the solar system, such as Saturn (pictured). But why? Work your way through the maze to find out. When you find the exit route, it will lead you to the correct answer.

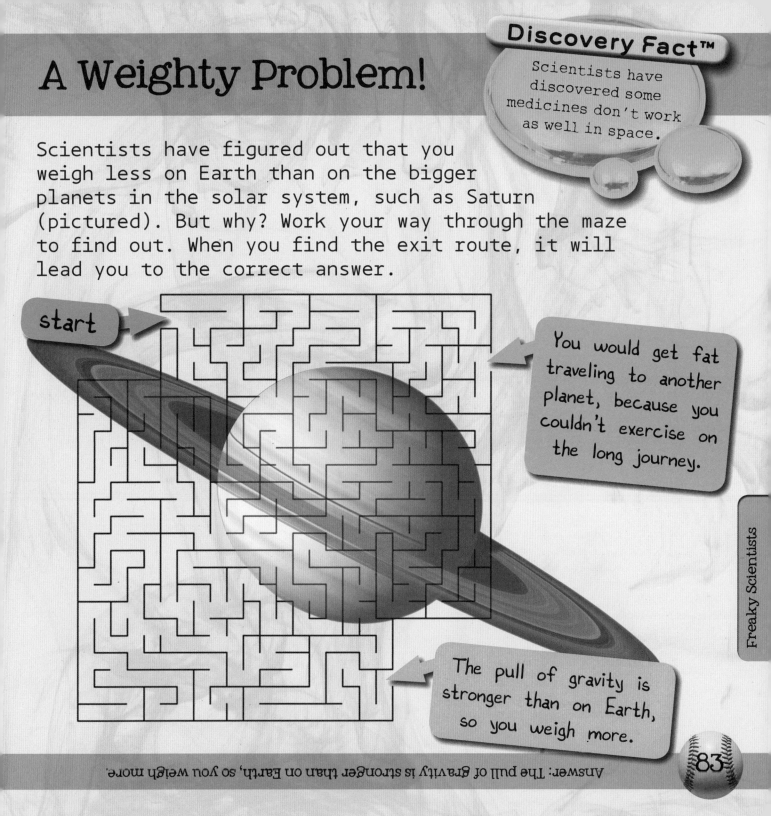

start

You would get fat traveling to another planet, because you couldn't exercise on the long journey.

The pull of gravity is stronger than on Earth, so you weigh more.

Freaky Scientists

Answer: The pull of gravity is stronger than on Earth, so you weigh more.

Space Junk!

We humans can make a mess just about anywhere—even in space. Crack the code to find out how many pieces of man-made space junk are orbiting Earth.

z	y	x	w	v	u	t	s	r	q	p	o	n	m	l	k	j	i	h	g	f	e	d	c	b	a
a	b	c	d	e	f	g	h	i	j	k	l	m	n	o	p	q	r	s	t	u	v	w	x	y	z

l	e	v	i		l	m	v		n	r	o	o	r	l	m

Discovery Fact™

Space junk is made up of old parts of rockets, satellites, paint flakes, dust, and waste from rocket engines.

Man on the Moon!

On July 20, 1969, at 10:56 p.m., astronauts Neil Armstrong and Buzz Aldrin made history by being the first humans to walk on the Moon. Answer the questions in the crossword puzzle, then read down the gray box to find out the name of their spacecraft.

		1.									
		P									
	2.										
		L									
3.											
		4.									
		11									

1. **Person who works and travels in space.**
2. **Large rocky body that orbits Earth.**
3. **The last name of the third member of the "moon walk" crew.**
   (Clue: Look at the DiscoveryFact™!)
4. **The path a planet travels on.**

Albert Einstein is one of the most famous scientists ever. But when he was a boy, what did he say when his mom told him that his new baby sister would be nice to play with? Crack the code to find out!

z	y	x	w	v	u	t	s	r	q	p	o	n	m	l	k	j	i	h	g	f	e	d	c	b	a
a	b	c	d	e	f	g	h	i	j	k	l	m	n	o	p	q	r	s	t	u	v	w	x	y	z

b	v	h		y	f	g		d	s	v	i	v		z	i	v

r	g	h		d	s	v	v	o	h

Einstein lived from 1879 to 1955. In 1999, *Time* magazine named him person of the century.

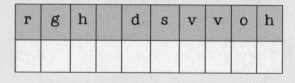

Discovery Fact™

Einstein thought of his Theory of Relativity by looking in a mirror and wondering if his reflection would vanish if he traveled faster than light.

Answer: Yes, but where are its wheels?

Under the Ocean!

Scientist William Beebe and diver Otis Barton wanted to study ocean life deep beneath the ocean waves. So, in 1930, they did the obvious thing—they invented a big, metal diving ball to sit in. Read around this word circle to find out its name. The first letter of the word is the letter in the center of the circle.

E A T
R B H
E Y
H P S

_ _ _ _ _ _ _ _ _ _ _ _

Freaky Scientists

87

Underwater House!

Marine biologist Jacques Cousteau took life underwater very seriously. So seriously, in fact, that he designed and built something rather unusual in the Red Sea. To find out what, unscramble the letters below, and fill in the spaces to finish the sentence.

Ⓐ **RUNDREATEW**

Ⓑ **EOUSH**

He built an

(A) _ _ _ _ _ _ _ _ _ _ _

(B) _ _ _ _ _ .

Answer: He built an underwater house.

Amazing Robots!

Robot engineers created an elephant-shape robot called Dasubee the "urinal elephant" to clean toilets in Kobe airport, Japan. Dasubee saves water by cleaning in mega-quick time, but just how fast is he? Solve this number puzzle to discover how many seconds Dasubee takes to scrub a toilet.

$$100 - 50 - 35 + 5 - 10 = \boxed{}$$

Answer: $\boxed{}$ seconds

Discovery Fact™

There's a robot called Roboflush that says, "Thank you," and flushes when you get off the toilet!

Mad Scientists!

Many great scientists have been crazy as well as brilliant. Follow the lines to match each scientist to their weird behavior!

A. Naturalist Charles Darwin

B. Henry Cavendish, discoverer of the gas hydrogen (pictured)

C. Physicist Richard Feynman

1. Wrote complex physic equations on bar mats

2. Kept 10,000 pet barnacles.

3. Dressed in clothes that were at least a century out of date.

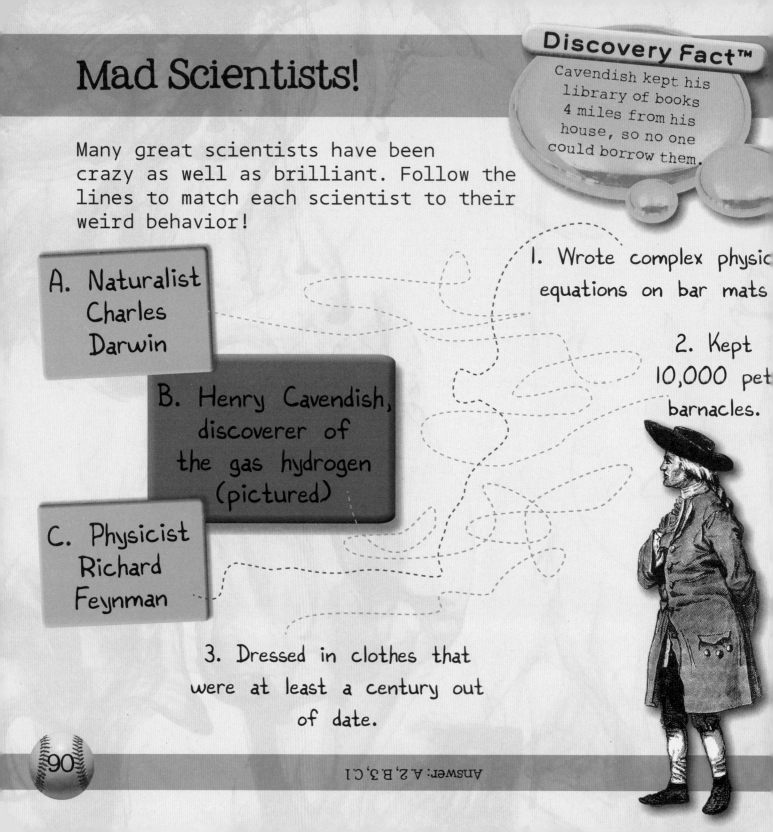

Answer: A.2, B.3, C.1

Tiny Robots?

Scientists believe they will soon be able to create incredibly small robots from just a teeny-tiny molecule or two, able to do all kinds of jobs. Crack the code below to discover the name of this amazing new technology.

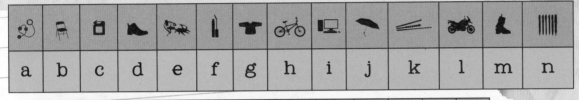

a	b	c	d	e	f	g	h	i	j	k	l	m	n

o	p	q	r	s	t	u	v	w	x	y	z

---- ---- ---- ---- ---- ---- ---- ---- ---- ---- ---- ---- ---- ----

Discovery Fact™

There is already a robot small enough to enter the body through a small slit to perform operations.

Medical nanobots could find and destroy red blood cells infected with dangerous germs.

Freaky Scientists

Answer: Nanotechnology

Let's Go Surfing!

British computer scientist Thomas Berners-Lee found a way to collect billions of information files held on computers all around the world. This crazy dude developed software as a way of linking all this information together on the Internet. Read around the word circles below to discover what the term "www" in website addresses means. The first letter of each word is the letter in the center of the circle.

http://www

D O W L R

E I W D

B W E

_ _ _ _ _   _ _ _ _   _ _ _

Answer: World wide web

Ahead of His Time!

Not all scientific geniuses get the recognition they deserve when they are alive. In 1822, mathematician Charles Babbage invented the very first version of a device that we use every day in the modern world—but it was never built. Unscramble the letters below to discover what it was.

ROMEPUCT

___ ___ ___ ___ ___ ___ ___ ___

Discovery Fact™

The first fully programmable electronic computer was built in the U.S. by John Eckert and John Mauchly in 1946.

Freaky Scientists

Weird Science!

In 1997, scientists successfully grew a human ear on the back of a mouse. The ear could safely be removed without the mouse dying. Why did they do such a weird thing? Work your way through the maze to find out. When you find the exit route, it will lead you to the correct answer!

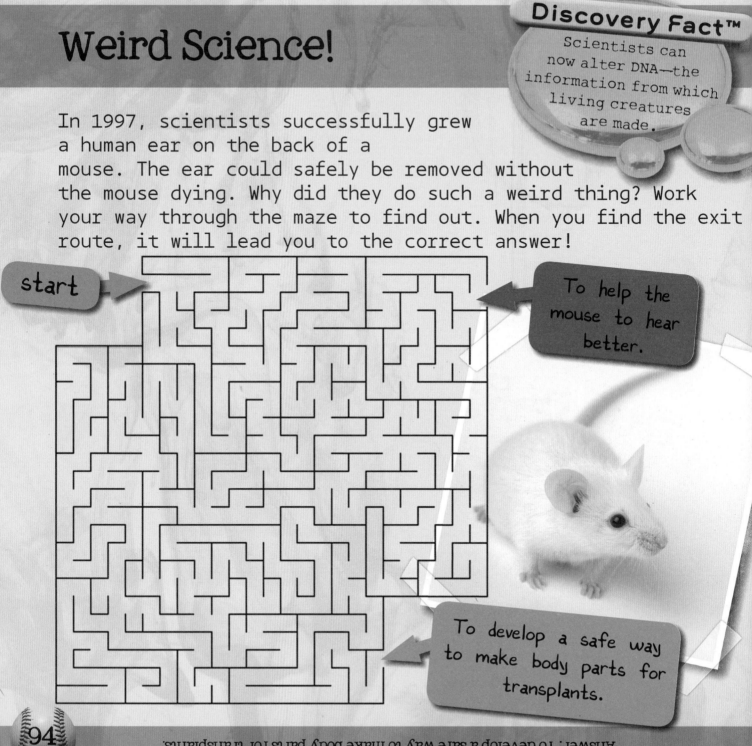

start

To help the mouse to hear better.

To develop a safe way to make body parts for transplants.

Answer: To develop a safe way to make body parts for transplants.

Need a Change?

If changing your hairstyle is not enough, doctors can operate on you to alter the way you look! They can make you fatter or thinner, look younger or older, or even change your skin color. Unscramble the letters below to figure out the special name these doctors have.

CLASTIP UGEROSNS

_ _ _ _ _ _ _   _ _ _ _ _ _ _ _

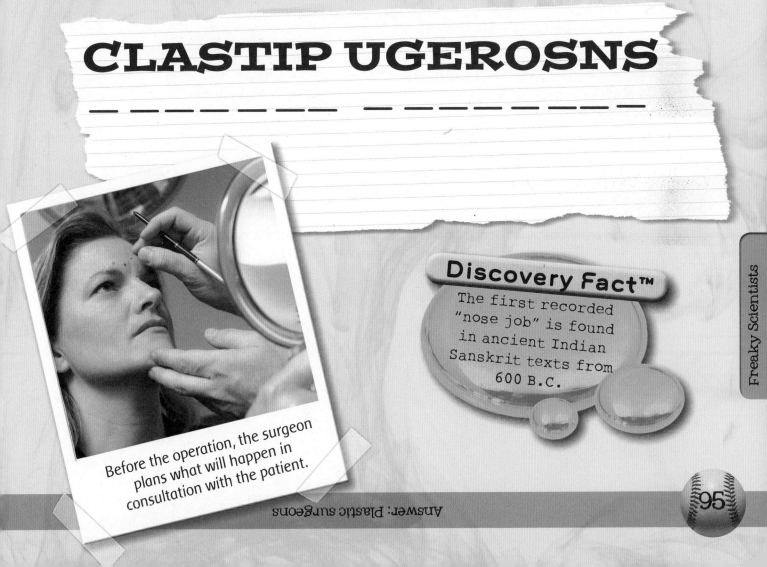

Before the operation, the surgeon plans what will happen in consultation with the patient.

Discovery Fact™

The first recorded "nose job" is found in ancient Indian Sanskrit texts from 600 B.C.

Freaky Scientists

Acknowledgments

Front cover: c Martin Mistretta/Getty, tr d8/Scott Rothstein, bl Dreamstime.com/Antonio Ballesteros, bc Handke-Neu/Corbis, br Hulton-Deutsch Collection/Corbis

Back cover: t Martin Mistretta/Getty, b Dreamstime.com/Rafael Laguillo

1 Dreamstime.com/Antonio Ballesteros, 2 tl Dreamstime.com/Kristian Sekulic, tr Dreamstime.com/Scott Rothstein, 2 br Bronwyn8/istockphoto.com, p3 tr LDF/istockphoto.com, 3 bl NASA, 3 br wrangle/ istockphoto.com, 4 Dreamstime.com/Antonio Ballesteros, 5 Rcpphot/Dreamstime.com, 6 Dreamstime.com/Eti Swinford, 7 Dreamstime.com/Steve Degenhardt, 8 Dreamstime.com, 9 Michael Nicholson/Corbis, 10 Richard Melloul/Sygma/Corbis, 11 claudiodivizia//istockphoto.com, 12 Dreamstime.com/Ewa Walicka, 13 Hulton/Deutsch Collection/Corbis, 14 mura/istockphoto.com, 15 Siemonet Ronald/Corbis Sygma, 16 mb8007/ istockphoto.com, 17 Andyd/istockphoto.com, 18 Dreamstime.com/Michael Shake, 19 Bettmann/Corbis, 20 Dreamstime.com/Scott Rothstein, 21 Dreamstime.com/Lynn Baxter, 23 Dreamstime.com, 24 Dreamstime.com/Olaf Schlueter, 25 wrangle/ istockphoto. com,, 26 Reuters/Corbis, 27 mikheewnick/istockphoto.com,, 28 Dreamstime.com/Kristian Sekulic, 29 Dreamstime.com/Lee Reitz, 30 Dreamstime.com/Eldoronki, 32 Richard A. Cooke/Corbis, 33 Bettmann/Corbis, 34 Dreamstime.com/Vladimirs, 35 Jon Feingersh/zefa/Corbis, 36 Dreamstime.com/Yuen Che Chia, 37 Dreamstime.com, 38 thinair28/istockphoto.com, 39 Dreamstime. com/Ewa Walicka, 40 Bronwyn8/istockphoto.com, 41 Visuals Unlimited/Corbis, 42 Dreamstime.com/Kati Neudert, 43 Dr. Milton Reisch/Corbis, 44 Dreamstime.com/Scott Rothstein, 45 Dreamstime.com/Ljupco Smokovski, 46 Paul Souders/Corbis, 47 Christophe Boisvieux/Corbis, 48 Jon Hughes and Russell Gooday, 49 felinda/istockphoto.com, 50 LemonCrumpet/Sharealike, 51 Hedda Gjerpen/istockphoto.com, 52 David Monniaux/GNU, 53 Dreamstime.com/Rachel Burnside, 54 Allkindza/ istockphoto. com, 55 Giorgio Fochesato/istockphoto, 56 rogerpilkington/ istockphoto.com, 57 Veni/ istockphoto.com, 58 Dreamstime.com/ Patti Gray, 59 Andyworks/ istockphoto.com, 60 Ratsuben/istockphoto, 61 Dale Hogan/ istockphoto.com, 62 Duncan Walker/ istockphoto.com, 63 Bettmann/Corbis, 64 Corbis, 65 Jose Antonio Santiso/ istockphoto.com, 66 Jan Prchal/ istockphoto.com, 67 jailfree/istockphoto.com, 68 Iryna Kurhan/istockphoto.com, 69 Borg Mesch, 70 Oleg Prikhodko/istockphoto.com, 71 Dario Rota/ istockphoto.com, 72 Steven Wynn/istockphoto.com, 73 ranplett/istockphoto.com, 74 Dreamstime.com/Alina Isakovich, 75 millerpd/istockphoto, 76 Dreamstime.com/Steve Luker, 77 Dreamstime.com/Fdbphotography, 78 Sergei Didyk/istockphoto.com, 79 Rob Broek/ istockphoto.com, 80 Dreamstime.com/Kirsty Pargeter, 81 NASA, 82 Ken Brown/istockphoto.com, 83 NASA, 84 NASA, 85 NASA, 86 Bettmann/Corbis, 87 Ralph White/Corbis, 88 Doxa, 89 Susan Law Cain/istockphoto.com, 90 Bettmann/ Corbis, 91 Dreamstime.com/Billyfoto, 92 zack/istockphoto.com, 93 LDF/istockphoto.com, 94 dra_schwartz/istockphoto.com, 95 Dennis Guyitt/istockphoto.com